Copyright © Chris Beetles Ltd 2012

Chris Beetles Fine Photographs

3-5 Swallow Street

London

W1B 4DE

020 7434 4319

gallery@chrisbeetles.com

www.chrisbeetlesfinephotographs.com

ISBN 978-1-905738-49-6

Compiled and edited by Giles Huxley-Parlour

Written by Giles Huxley-Parlour and Alexandra Mackay

Design by Jeremy Brook of Graphic Ideas

Colour separation and printing by Geoff Neal Litho

Front cover: Cecil Beaton, *Queen Elizabeth II Coronation Portrait, 2 June 1953* [41]

Front endpaper: Jacques-Henri Lartigue, *My Cousin Bichonnade, Paris, 1905* [26]

Contents frontispiece: Irving Penn, *Fashion Photograph, (Vogue Cover), New York, 1951* [56]

Back endpaper: Steve McCurry, *Road to Jalalabad, Afghanistan, 1992* [88]

Back cover: Herman Leonard, *'Prez' Lester Young, NYC, 1948* [65]

THE PHOTOGRAPHERS
2012

 CHRIS BEETLES FINE PHOTOGRAPHS

CONTENTS

ADOLPHE BRAUN Jean Adolphe Braun (1811-1877)

For a biography of Adolphe Braun, please refer to *The Photographers 2011*, page 18

1 ZURICH AND THE ALPS, SWITZERLAND, CIRCA 1885
Inscribed with title on mount
Carbon print, mounted on board, printed circa 1885
14 x 18 ½ inches

ROBERT CRAWSHAY Robert Thompson Crawshay (1817-1879)

Robert Thompson Crawshay was born on 3 March 1817, the grandson of Richard Crawshay, the 'Iron King of Wales'. His grandfather had worked his way up from poverty to own one of the largest iron works in the world, and the family was immensely wealthy, living at Cyfarthfa Castle, Methyr Tydfil, Wales. He was educated at Dr Pritchard's School in Llandaff, and then worked for the family firm, becoming the head of the business on his father's death in 1867. He was a well-liked and successful businessman, at one point employing over 5000 people. In his spare time Crawshay developed an interest in photography, becoming a proficient and prolific amateur. He won many prizes for his photographs during the 1870s, particularly from the Photographic Society (later the Royal Photographic Society). He died on a trip to Cheltenham on 10 May 1879.

GHP

2 CAUGHT 30 OCTOBER, 1875

Signed, inscribed with title and the weights of each fish on mount

Albumen print, mounted on board, printed circa 1875

9 x 14 inches

HENRY DIXON (1820-1892)

For a biography of Henry Dixon, please refer to *The Photographers 2011*, page 22.

3 ELEPHANT AND KEEPER, LONDON ZOO, CIRCA 1885
Inscribed 'Elephant d'Afrique' on reverse
Carbon print, printed circa 1885
9 ½ x 12 ¾ inches

WILLIAM ENGLAND (1830-1896)

William England was an early British photographer, who came of age during the dawn of photography in the 1840s. He went on to be the chief photographer for the London Stereoscopic Company during the 1850s and 60s.

William England was born in Trowbridge, Wiltshire and became an apprentice in a local daguerreotype studio at the age of 12. England moved to London in the late 1840s to further a career in photography, and married Rosalie Vernier in 1850. In 1854 he joined the London Stereoscope Company (becoming the London Stereoscopic Company in 1856), a leading business selling stereoscopic prints – a popular collectable at the time.

England quickly became one of their most successful and admired photographers, travelling all over Europe and America to take images for the company. In 1858 he photographed the famous acrobat, Charles Blondin, tightrope walking across the Niagara Falls. It became the best selling stereograph of all time, selling more than 100,000 copies world-wide.

In the mid 1860s he founded his own photographic business, continuing to travel around Europe and build on his reputation as a landscape photographer. He was a member of the Photographic Society (later The Royal Photographic Society) from 1863, a founder member of The Solar Club in 1866 and President of West London Photographic Society in 1888-89.

William England died in Kensington, London, on 13 August 1896.

GHP

4 PANORAMA VIEW OF MURREN, SWITZERLAND, CIRCA 1862
Inscribed with title and dedication to The Alpine Club on mount
Albumen print, mounted on board,
printed circa 1862
6 ¼ x 8 ¼ inches

ARTHUR DEBENHAM (1845-1936)

Arthur Debenham was a successful photographer based in Ryde on the Isle of Wight. He was the son of a photographer, Samuel Debenham, and became an apprentice at the London School of Photography for four years from 1859. He went on to open studios in Ryde, Brighton, Southsea and London. His sitters included King Edward VII, and Nicholas II of Russia during his last visit to England in 1910. GHP

5 YACHT IN
FULL SAIL,
COWES,
ISLE OF WIGHT,
ENGLAND,
CIRCA 1895
Stamped with
photographer's
copyright blind stamp
Inscribed 'J Hetes'
on reverse
Silver gelatin print,
printed circa 1895
9 ¼ x 11 ¼ inches

FRANK MEADOW SUTCLIFFE Francis Meadow Sutcliffe (1853-1941)

Frank Meadow Sutcliffe was a groundbreaking and influential photographer, known for vehemently promoting photography as an art form. He is particularly known for his genre scenes of Whitby in Yorkshire, where he lived and worked for most of his life.

Francis Meadow Sutcliffe was born in Leeds on 6 October 1853, the son of Thomas Sutcliffe, the celebrated watercolourist and his wife, Sarah Button. He was the eldest of eight children and was educated at a local 'dame school' until the age of 14, when his father fell ill and he was sent to work as a clerk at Tetley's brewery. On his father's return to health eighteen months later the family moved to Ewe Cote Hall, near Whitby, and Sutcliffe became interested in photography. He received his first camera in 1869 – a large, mahogany device that used 15x12 inch glass plates.

His father died when Sutcliffe was 18 and, as the only potential breadwinner in his large family, he became a full-time photographer. He won photographic commissions through some of his late father's connections, including Francis Frith who paid him to photograph local abbeys for his postcard business, and the celebrated art critic, John Ruskin, who commissioned him to photograph the grounds of his house in 1873. However, these intermittent assignments did not generate enough income so, in 1873, Sutcliffe moved to Tunbridge Wells to open a portrait studio. It was a financial failure and he returned to Whitby in 1875 to open a studio there with his new wife, Eliza.

This set-up, which moved to larger premises in 1894, was to provide Sutcliffe with a steady income until 1922. It also enabled him to take the photographs for which he became best known – highly finished, atmospheric views of Whitby and its inhabitants. The photographs were taken for his own pleasure and are celebrated for their immaculate compositions and technical virtuosity, a difficult feat with cumbersome 19th century equipment. By the 1890s Sutcliffe had won many international competitions with his images of Whitby, as well as becoming a regular voice in the British photographic community, writing for publications including *Amateur Photographer*. In 1892 he joined a group of photographers called 'The Linked Ring', founded by Henry Peach Robinson that same year with the aim of promoting photography as a fine art.

In 1922 he closed his studio in Whitby and retired a minor local celebrity, becoming curator of the Whitby Literary and Philosophical Society. He was made a Fellow of The Royal Photographic Society in 1935, and died at his home in Sleights on 31 May 1941. GHP

12

6 MAN WITH HUNTING DOGS, 1880s
Platinum print, printed 1880s
5 ¾ x 7 ¾ inches

PETER HENRY EMERSON Pedro Enrique Emerson (1856-1936)

For a biography of Peter Henry Emerson, please refer to *The Photographers 2010*, page 7.

7 HAYMAKER WITH RAKE, NORFOLK, CIRCA 1895
Photogravure, printed circa 1895
11 x 7 ¾ inches
Illustrated: Peter Henry Emerson, *Pictures of East Anglian Life*, 1888, plate 31

14

8 COL BOILEAU AND TIGER, 1880s
Inscribed with title on reverse
Albumen print, printed 1880s
6 x 4 ½ inches

9 GOLFER AT
NORTH BERWICK,
27 AUGUST, 1881
Dated and inscribed
'N Berwick' on reverse
Albumen print, printed
circa 1881
6 x 5 inches

16

10 THREE-PART PANORAMA OF ST PETER PORT, GUERNSEY, CIRCA 1865

3 x Albumen prints, printed circa 1865

Each is approximately 10 ½ x 14 inches

11 THREE YACHTS AT COWES, ISLE OF WIGHT, ENGLAND, CIRCA 1895

Inscribed 'Hex, Fulatea and Sara' on reverse

Silver gelatin print, printed circa 1895

8 x 10 ½ inches

ALFRED STIEGLITZ (1864-1946)

Alfred Stieglitz is arguably the most significant figure in the history of American photography. Stieglitz's career spanned almost 50 years, during which he championed the medium and called for the recognition of its artistic merits alongside painting and sculpture. Stieglitz also became renowned as a successful writer and as a pioneering gallery owner showing European painting and photography.

Alfred Stieglitz was born in Hoboken, New Jersey, on 1 January 1864. His parents were German-Jewish immigrants and his father, Edward Stieglitz, had made a substantial fortune in the cloth industry. In 1871 he enrolled his son at the Charlier Institute, the best private school in New York. Ten years later Stieglitz moved to Germany, where he studied to be an engineer at the Königlich Technische Hochschule in Berlin. While studying in Berlin, he met Hermann Vogel, the acclaimed photo-chemist, who had a great influence upon him, and sparked his interest in photography. Vogel taught him many of the technical elements of photography, and introduced him to the photogravure technique. Stieglitz purchased his first camera and travelled through Europe to photograph the daily life of people in the cities, as well as landscapes and street scenes. In 1887 he won his first award for his work in an amateur photography competition, and several German and English magazines began to publish his photographs.

In 1890, his sister Flora died, and his family urged him to return to New York. His father's money helped him buy a small photoengraving business, and he began to regularly contribute essays on photography and photographic technique to *The American Amateur Photographer*. He became a co-editor of the publication in 1893 and that same year married Emmeline Obermeyer, a woman who was wealthy in her own right. It was a marriage of financial convenience and it allowed him to focus on his photography and writing, rather than business. In 1896 he oversaw the merging of the two photographic societies of New York.

Photogravure

Photogravure is a photomechanical means of printing images from photographic negatives. There are several stages to the making of a photogravure. First, a tissue covered on one side with bichromated gelatin is exposed to light under a transparent positive. The tissue is then firmly pressed down onto a copper plate, to transfer the gelatin onto the surface of the plate. The copper plate, now covered in gelatin from the tissue, is then placed in an etching bath filled with chemicals, which begin to erode the metal surface. The erosion occurs to varying degrees, depending on the thickness of the gelatin. Having been removed from the etching bath, the copper plate is then ready to be inked. Once inked the plate is used to print the image onto high quality printing paper, much like an etching.

12 A DIRIGIBLE, 1910
Photogravure, printed 1911
7 x 7 inches

The Society of Amateur Photographers and The New York Camera Club became The Camera Club of New York, with Stieglitz as its vice-president. The following year the first issue of *Camera Notes*, the club's magazine, was published. As the editor, Stieglitz controlled the content and the design of the magazine. He was meticulous about every detail, and the magazine was published to the highest standard. The photogravures were printed on the finest paper and Stieglitz wrote many opinionated articles for its pages.

Stieglitz remained vice-president of the club for five years, during which time his photographic work became increasingly popular. By 1902, some members of the group were growing tired of Stieglitz's autocratic ruling of the club. Stieglitz to, was frustrated that his artistic and aesthetic ideas were not being adhered too and therefore formed a new photographic club, the Photo-Secessionists, with a few like-minded members of the old club. Most notable of these was Edward Steichen, who he had met in 1900, and who had become a close friend. In 1905 Steichen acquired for the group an exhibition space on Fifth Avenue, which they called The Little Galleries of the Photo-Secession. In November 1905, the first exhibition of their work opened; it included many of Stieglitz and Steichen's own photographs, as well as the art of the Pictorialists from France, Britain, Austria and Germany. Pictorialism was a word used to describe the work of certain photographers working in the late 1800s whose chief aim was to create atmospheric fine art photography, often printed on platinum plates. Stieglitz's early photography was characterised by this soft-focus aesthetic. His early masterpieces, *Winter – Fifth Avenue* and *The Terminal,* were taken on a large format (8x10 inch) camera and show Stieglitz's preoccupation with atmosphere. Stieglitz also managed the publication of a magazine for the group, *Camera Work,* which was first published in 1905. Steichen greatly influenced Stieglitz's view of art and, from 1908 onwards, the exhibitions at the gallery focused less and less on photography and more on modern art from America and Europe – indeed he was one of the first gallery owners in America to include work by John Marin, Arthur Dove, Picasso, Matisse and Rodin in his exhibitions.

By the start of the First World War Steichen and Stieglitz's collaboration had come to an end as their opinions of photography had altered. Whereas Steichen continued in the Pictorialist tradition, Stieglitz, who was heavily influenced by the modern art that he displayed on the walls of the gallery, began to focus on form in his photography rather than atmosphere. He strongly believed that photography was the perfect medium to represent modern life and that emphasizing the qualities particular to the medium was crucial for photographic advancement. This change in his photography is demonstrated in, *The Steerage*, Stieglitz's signature photograph, taken in 1907 but not published until 1917. Stieglitz described it as having all the qualities of a modern photograph. Taken on board a steamer travelling from New York to Bremen in Germany, this photograph depicts the separation of the classes in travel, as the upper-class travellers look down onto the poorer passengers in their cramped conditions. In 1917 Stieglitz closed the gallery and published the final issue of *Camera Work*, dedicated entirely to Steichen.

In 1916 Stieglitz met the American artist Georgia O'Keefe. The pair corresponded for the next two years and in 1918, when O'Keefe moved to New York, Stieglitz began a series of photographs of her. In total Stieglitz took over 100 photos of the artist in the first year of their acquaintance. The series is some of his most famous work and includes full portraits, nudes and close up images of her head and hands. This period of Stieglitz's career was particularly productive and in 1922 he produced another important series of images, *Equivalents*, which he took on a handheld 4 x 5 inch camera. The series, which consists of over 200 photographs, entirely of clouds, was taken over a period of a few years, mostly at Lake George, where the Stieglitz family had their summer home.

Stieglitz married O'Keefe in 1924, after his divorce from Obermeyer was finalised. He took full control of the promotion of O'Keefe's work and dedicated many magazine publishings and exhibitions to her paintings. In 1926 he opened a new gallery, which he named, The Intimate Gallery. In 1927, he met Dorothy Norman, who was visiting the gallery, and who soon became his lover, while O'Keefe spent most of her time in New Mexico. For the first three decades of the 20th Century, Stieglitz had tried to advance the status of photography in the art world. In 1928 he achieved a breakthrough, when the Metropolitan Museum of Art accepted his gift of 28 prints of his work, and dedicated a room in the museum to photography. In 1929 his gallery was forced to close, and he was left without a place to display his pictures. His close friend, Paul Strand, also a photographer, began to raise money to buy Stieglitz a new gallery, which he opened in late 1929 and named An American Place.

After a few years of inactivity in his own photographic production, Stieglitz began a new project at the beginning of the 1930s, which returned to his early subject matter of New York City. In this series however, instead of taking his pictures from the street, he photographed the streets of New York from the window of his apartment in the Shelton Hotel, and from the window of An American Place. His objective was to photograph the citizens of New York's interaction with the modern city. This was the last major photographic project that Stieglitz undertook, returning to focus on business at the gallery for the final years of his life.

Having suffered a series of heart attacks, Stieglitz died in New York on 13 July 1946. Upon his death, O'Keefe took up the task of organising his estate. She bequeathed many of his prints and work he had collected by other artists and photographers to galleries and museums in America, such as the Museum of Modern Art, the Art Institute of Chicago and the Boston Museum of Fine Art. Stieglitz is remembered as one of the most important figures in modern art, not only as a photographer, but also as a collector and writer on photography and aesthetics. His galleries exhibited some of the most celebrated figures in modern art, and held some of the first exhibitions of photographers such as Ansel Adams. His own work is some of the most important in 20th century photography, and his contribution to the stylistic and technical advancement of the medium is probably unparalleled.

AM

13 THE HAND OF MAN, 1902
Photogravure, printed 1911
6 ¼ x 8 ½ inches

14 LOWER MANHATTAN, 1910

Photogravure, printed 1911

6 ¼ x 7 ¾ inches

15 THE MAURETANIA, 1910
Photogravure, printed 1911
8 ¼ x 6 ¼ inches

HERBERT PONTING Herbert George Ponting FRGS (1870-1935)

Herbert Ponting was renowned for his meticulous and adventurous approach to photography. His most famous work was taken during The British Antarctic Expedition 1910-1913, when he became the first professional photographer to capture the Antarctic.

Herbert Ponting was born in Salisbury, Wiltshire, on 21 March 1870. He was the son of Francis W Ponting, a successful banker, a career that his father hoped his son would follow. On leaving school, he took a job at a bank in Liverpool. However, in 1892, he gave up his position and travelled to the West Coast of America. There he met his future wife, Mary Biddle Eliott, whom he married in 1895. With the help of his family's money, Ponting bought a farm in California, which subsequently failed and they returned to England six years later.

After only a short period of time, however, Ponting chose to return to the United States, at which point he grew interested in photography and chose to make a career from it. An acquaintance commenting on one of his stereoscopic photographs suggested to Ponting that he approach publishing companies, as well as entering his work into photographic competitions. In 1901, he travelled to the Far East to photograph the people, landscapes, and wildlife of various countries including Burma and Japan. The results were published in several magazines, including *Harpers Bazaar,* and *The Illustrated London News.* Ponting's first book: *In Lotus Land, Japan* was published in 1910, by which time he had an established reputation as a successful photographer.

In 1910, Ponting set sail with Captain Robert Falcon Scott's British Antarctic Expedition as the official photographer, personally chosen by Scott. His established reputation and his connection with Cecil Meares, who was in charge of the dogs for the expedition, had helped Ponting acquire the post. *The Geographical Journal* wrote at the time, 'The British Antarctic Expedition should be very well served by the camera in Mr Ponting's hands.' Ponting's images from the trip are now world

famous, and form one of the great bodies of Polar exploration photography. Using a plate camera and glass-plate negatives, Ponting overcame almost impossible conditions to record daily life on the expedition. Happy to risk life and limb to achieve the pictures he wanted, he would then process the film in his makeshift darkroom at their camp in Cape Evans. Diaries from the expedition document that Ponting went to great lengths to take the best photograph, on one occasion narrowly avoiding an attack by Killer whales. Ponting was well liked by his colleagues, but he maintained a distance from them, instead focusing on his photography with painstaking detail.

Herbert Ponting left the expedition in February 1912 and returned to England. Scott famously succumbed to the harsh environment soon afterwards in March 1912, on his trek back from the South Pole – deflated from having been beaten to his goal by the Norwegian explorer, Roald Amundsen.

On his return to England Ponting was disappointed by the lack of response to his photographs and films. Hearing of the subsequent deaths of Scott and the four other men who reached the pole, he set out to promote the legacy of the expedition, rather than focusing on new projects. He held several lectures, and produced the film, *Great White Silence*, which received great acclaim.

In the last few years of his life, Ponting turned away from photography, investing in business ventures, which made him very little money. At the time of his death in London, 1935, he was almost destitute. Herbert Ponting is remembered as a technically skilled photographer, and his photographs have become crucial in establishing both the legacy of Robert Scott and the memory of his polar exploits.

AM

16 LANTERNS AT SUMIYOSHI TEMPLE, OSAKA, JAPAN, 1904

Signed, dated and inscribed with photographer's copyright details

Inscribed with title on reverse

Carbon print, printed circa 1904

19 ½ x 13 ¾ inches

17 NANTAI ZAN, JAPAN, 1904

Signed, dated and inscribed with photographer's copyright details

Inscribed with title on reverse

Carbon print, printed circa 1904

14 x 19 inches

18 WISTERIAS OF KAMEIDO, TOKYO, JAPAN, 1904

Signed, dated and inscribed with photographer's copyright details

Inscribed with title on reverse

Carbon print, printed circa 1904

13 ¾ x 18 ¾ inches

19 THE TERRA NOVA HELD UP IN THE PACK, 13 DECEMBER 1910

Stamped with Scott Polar Research Institute blind stamp

Numbered on reverse

Platinum print, printed 2012

20 x 14 inches

From an edition of 30

The Terra Nova Expedition

The British Antarctic Expedition, also called the Terra Nova Expedition (after its supply ship), was Robert Falcon Scott's second attempt to reach the South Pole, and has become infamous as a tragic, but heroic, story of polar exploration. Having failed to attain this goal on his original journey, the Discovery Expedition of 1901-1904, Scott once again attempted to reach the Pole in 1910, spurred on by the recent expedition of Ernest Shackleton, who came within 97 miles of achieving the perilous feat in January 1909. Once he had resolved to try again, Scott met with the Royal Geographical Society and looked for support from the government and other organisations to fund the expedition.

He was successful, and Scott set sail from London on 1 June 1910. The team headed south taking stock in Melbourne, Australia, and then New Zealand, before arriving at Ross Island, Antarctica, on 11 January 1911. Having settled there, news reached them of a second team, set up not far away, also attempting to reach the South Pole, led by the renowned explorer, Roald Amundsen. It had now become a race between two nations, Great Britain and Norway.

The expedition came well equipped, carrying with them advanced photographic and scientific equipment, along with the power of over 30 dogs and 20 horses, used to pull sledges and transport supplies during the team's march across the ice. Although reaching the Pole was his main objective, Scott's support teams also carried out scientific experiments and recorded findings of wildlife and the geographical surroundings of Antarctica – the expedition is remembered as pioneering for the information it amassed.

Despite travelling to Antarctica with a crew of over 30 men, Scott selected only four other men to actually accompany him to the Pole. On 4 January 1912, Edgar Evans, Edward Wilson, Lawrence Oates, Henry Bowers and Scott set off towards the polar plateau from Cape Evans. However, the expedition was destinedk to fail. On reaching the pole, on 17 January 1912, the five men discovered the flag and tent left behind by Amundsen's team, who reached the Pole five weeks earlier. This was a bitter disappointment to Scott, who had hoped to claim the victory in the name of the British Empire.

The very next day, they began the 800-mile return journey. With oncoming bad weather and the beginnings of exhaustion, the team started to deteriorate. Edgar Evans took a fatal blow to the head while descending the Beardmore Glacier, and died on 17 January 1912. Lawrence Oates, who was suffering from an injury sustained to his foot, chose to sacrifice himself in order for the remaining three men to make better progress. Scott noted in his diary that Oates got up and walked out of the tent into a blizzard saying, 'I am just going outside, and may be some time.' Scott made his final diary entry on 29 March 1912, when he asked for the families the men left behind be provided for. Their bodies were found eight months later during a search party, and a memorial was erected on the spot.

AM

20 GROTTO IN BERG, TERRA NOVA IN THE DISTANCE, 5 JANUARY 1911
Stamped with Scott Polar Research Institute blind stamp
Numbered on reverse
Platinum print, printed 2012
20 x 14 inches
From an edition of 30

21 VIEW OF THE DECK ON THE TERRA NOVA WITH DOGS, FROM ENGINE ROOM HATCH, 3 JANUARY 1911

Stamped with Scott Polar Research Institute blind stamp

Numbered on reverse

Platinum print, printed 2012

20 x 14 inches

From an edition of 30

22 BEAUTIFUL BROKEN ICE, REFLECTIONS AND THE TERRA NOVA, 7 JANUARY 1911

Stamped with Scott Polar Research Institute blind stamp

Numbered on reverse

Platinum print, printed 2012

20 x 14 inches

From an edition of 30

23 CAPTAIN SCOTT, 13 APRIL 1911
Stamped with Scott Polar Research Institute blind stamp
Numbered on reverse
Platinum print, printed 2012
20 x 14 inches
From an edition of 30

24 THE TERRA NOVA STUCK IN THE PACK, 13 DECEMBER 1910

Stamped with Scott Polar Research Institute blind stamp

Numbered on reverse

Platinum print, printed 2012

20 x 14 inches

From an edition of 30

EDWARD STEICHEN Edward Jean Steichen (1879-1973)

For a biography of Edward Steichen, please refer to *The Photographers 2011*, page 24.

25 GARY COOPER,
HOLLYWOOD, 1930
Signed by George Tice and Joanna
Steichen on photographer's estate
label on reverse
Silver gelatin print, printed later
13 x 10 ½ inches

JACQUES-HENRI LARTIGUE (1894-1986)

For a biography of Jacques-Henri Lartigue, please refer to *The Photographers 2010*, page 20.

The three photographs included here illustrate Lartigue's principal photographic interest – the camera's ability to freeze time. By the early 20th century, portable cameras had become commonplace, thanks in part to Kodak's famous, hand-held 'Brownie' camera. Although he did not use a Brownie himself, Lartigue, and other photographers of his time, took advantage of the faster shutter-speeds that enabled these cameras to be hand-held, and used them to make images that had simply not been possible before. They were suddenly able to become masters of time and movement. Lartigue's photographs capture his wealthy friends and family at leisure, and so have also become significant social documents of his class and era.

26 MY COUSIN BICHONNADE, PARIS, 1905
Signed and stamped with photographer's estate blind stamp
Silver gelatin print, printed later
9 ½ x 13 ¼ inches

27 WHEELED BOBSLEIGH INVENTED BY JACQUES LARTIGUE, 1911
Signed with photographer's initials, inscribed with title and dated 1915 on reverse
Silver gelatin print, printed between 1954 and 1963
11 ¾ x 15 ½ inches

28 SUZANNE LENGLEN, NICE, FRANCE, 1915
Signed with photographer's initials, inscribed with title and dated 1915 on reverse
Silver gelatin print, printed circa 1963
11 ¾ x 15 ½ inches

ANDRE KERTESZ Kertész Andor (1894-1985)

For a biography of André Kertész, please refer to *The Photographers 2010*, page 14

29 LOST CLOUD,
NEW YORK, 1937
Stamped with photographer's estate
ink stamp on reverse
Silver gelatin print, printed circa 1980
9 ¾ x 7 inches

30 HOMING SHIP,
NEW YORK, 1944
Stamped with photographer's estate
ink stamp on reverse
Silver gelatin print, printed circa 1980
13 ¾ x 10 ½ inches

ANSEL ADAMS Ansel Easton Adams (1902-1984)

For a biography of Ansel Adams, please refer to *The Photographers 2010*, page 36.

This striking picture by Ansel Adams falls into a genre of imagery that was made popular during the 1930s by Adams' colleagues in the famous Group f/64 collective, which included Adams, Edward Weston, Imogen Cunningham and other significant photographers. Eschewing the atmospheric, painterly ambitions of the earlier Pictorialists, these photographic pioneers championed clear, unfussy images that had an overtly Modernist aesthetic. Sharp-focused images of found objects and the natural world dominated their efforts and this image, taken later in 1950, illustrates Adams' position as their greatest exponent.

31 SEQUOIA ROOTS, MARIPOSA GROVE, YOSEMITE NATIONAL PARK, CALIFORNIA, 1950
Signed on mount
Affixed with portfolio label and numbered 79 on reverse of mount
Silver gelatin print, mounted on board, printed circa 1963
9 ½ x 7 ½ inches
From Portfolio Four, Ansel Adams, *What Majestic Word*, San Francisco: The Sierra Club, 1963

32 DUNES OCEANO, CALIFORNIA, 1963

Signed on mount

Affixed with portfolio label and numbered 79 on reverse of mount

Silver gelatin print, mounted on board, printed circa 1963

7 ¼ x 7 ¾ inches

From Portfolio Four, Ansel Adams, *What Majestic Word*, San Francisco: The Sierra Club, 1963

BILL BRANDT Hermann Wilhelm Brandt (1904-1983)

For a biography of Bill Brandt, please refer to *The Photographers 2010*, page 80.

33 WILLY LOTT'S COTTAGE, FLATFORD MILL, SUFFOLK, 1976
Signed and numbered 11/100 on mount
Silver gelatin print, mounted on board, printed 1970s
11 ¼ x 12 ¼ inches
From an edition of 100

THE FORD HILL
COLLECTION

THE FORD HILL COLLECTION

The Ford Hill Collection of portraits of Queen Elizabeth II is one of the most remarkable groups of photographs ever assembled by a private collector. At just over 300 items it is far from the largest, but it is unique because of the sheer breadth of imagery – from her earliest official portraits, to recent pictures.

Ford Hill is an American pianist and retired music professor, currently living in Bellingham, Washington State. He began the collection in 1967 by writing to photographers such as Cecil Beaton and Yousuf Karsh, asking to buy prints of their portraits of the Queen. In the days before photographs became collectable, and therefore valuable, the photographers often obliged. Ford quickly expanded the project into a long-term curatorial exercise, aiming to put together a body of work that showed the Queen over a number of years.

Over 40 years later that project had blossomed into a major historical archive, and in 2010 Ford Hill donated 256 of his portraits to the National Portrait Gallery, London. Despite having one of the largest and most prestigious collections of photographs in the world, these were all images that the museum did not hold at the time – Hill had surpassed even their own efforts.

The 14 images that are in our current exhibition come from the part of the Ford Hill Collection that the National Portrait Gallery already held prints of, and are therefore amongst the most prestigious images that Hill had gathered.

With a few exceptions, these particular prints were made expressly for Ford Hill, by the photographer or their studio, between 1967 and 1963. Most are large and, crucially, signed. In the vast majority of cases this makes them extraordinarily rare objects, unique on the market today.

DOROTHY WILDING (1893-1976)

Dorothy Wilding was a pre-eminent female portrait photographer in London during the first half of the 20th century. Famed for both her society portraits and her nudes, she experienced a meteoric rise in fame and demand, culminating in her becoming the photographer of choice to the British Royal Family from 1937.

Dorothy Wilding was born in Longford, Gloucestershire, on 10 January 1893, the youngest of ten children. She was an unwanted child and, aged four, she was passed to a childless aunt who lived in Cheltenham. An early ambition to become an actress was quickly thwarted by her uncle, so Wilding settled on becoming a photographer, teaching herself the basic skills such as printing and retouching. She moved to London and became apprenticed to a photographic retoucher in Knightsbridge, before opening up her first studio in Portman Square in 1915.

Her photographic skill and steely ambition meant that she quickly became sought after by London society – a sitting with the Selfridge family in particular helped her star to climb. Her first Royal assignment was in 1927, when she photographed the young Prince George, who later became the Duke of Kent. By the 1930s she had moved premises to a large studio in Old Bond Street and in 1937 she photographed the

new King George VI and Queen Mary – a royal warrant following swiftly that same year.

In addition to her work for the Royal Family, Wilding had also become one of the preferred portrait photographers for the significant cultural and political figures of the day. This was aided by her opening a second studio in New York in the late 1930s, taking on an exhausting trans-Atlantic schedule in the process. Her sitters included Nancy Astor, Tallulah Bankhead, Noël Coward, Aldous Huxley, William Somerset Maugham and a host of other celebrated names. In 1952 Wilding was commissioned to photograph Queen Elizabeth II, shortly after her accession to the throne. The images were used for a series of well-known (and now very collectable) stamps.

Dorothy Wilding died on 9 February 1976 in relative obscurity, having closed her Old Bond Street studio in 1958. GHP

34 PRINCESS ELIZABETH IN HER SEA RANGER UNIFORM, 1943
Silver gelatin print, printed between 1967 and 1973
18 ¾ x 13 inches
Provenance: The Ford Hill Collection

DOROTHY WILDING

35 PRINCESS ELIZABETH IN HER UNIFORM FOR THE AUXILIARY TERRITORIAL SERVICE, 1945

Signed 'Dorothy Wilding, London' in the negative

Silver gelatin print, printed between 1967 and 1973

19 ¼ x 14 inches

Provenance: The Ford Hill Collection

36 PRINCESS ELIZABETH, WEDDING PORTRAIT, 1947
Silver gelatin print, printed between 1967 and 1973
19 ½ x 15 ½ inches
Provenance: The Ford Hill Collection

DOROTHY WILDING

37 PRINCESS ELIZABETH AND PHILIP MOUNTBATTEN, ENGAGEMENT PORTRAIT, 1947
Silver gelatin print, printed between 1967 and 1973
19 ½ x 14 inches
Provenance: The Ford Hill Collection

In 1952 Wilding was commissioned to photograph Queen Elizabeth II for a series of stamps, shortly after her accession to the throne in February of that year. There were two sittings, one in February and one in April – the present portrait hails from the earlier shoot in which she wears the elaborately named 'Girls of Great Britain and Ireland Tiara', given to her by her Grandmother, Queen Mary, on her wedding day in 1947. The palace subsequently decided that a tiara was inappropriate, and so scheduled a second shoot for April in which she was to wear the diamond diadem worn by Queen Victoria on all her stamps, including the Penny Black. This is the shoot that resulted in the final image for the stamps, published by the Royal Mail later that year.

38 QUEEN ELIZABETH II, FEBRUARY 1952
Silver gelatin print, printed between 1967 and 1973
19 ½ x 14 inches
Provenance: The Ford Hill Collection

DOROTHY WILDING

39 QUEEN ELIZABETH II, APRIL 1952
Silver gelatin print, printed between 1967 and 1973
17 ½ x 14 inches
Provenance: The Ford Hill Collection

CECIL BEATON

Sir Cecil Walter Hardy Beaton CBE (1904-1980)

For a biography of Cecil Beaton, please refer to *The Photographers*, 2010, page 42.

40 QUEEN ELIZABETH II AT PRINCESS MARGARET'S WEDDING, 6 MAY 1960
Signed
Silver gelatin print, printed between 1967 and 1973
19 x 15 inches
Provenance: The Ford Hill Collection

CECIL BEATON

41 QUEEN ELIZABETH II CORONATION PORTRAIT, 2 JUNE 1953 [I]
Signed
Silver gelatin print, printed between 1967 and 1973
19 ½ x 15 ½ inches
Provenance: The Ford Hill Collection

42 QUEEN ELIZABETH II CORONATION PORTRAIT, 2 JUNE 1953 [II]
Signed
Silver gelatin print, printed between 1967 and 1973
19 ½ x 15 ½ inches
Provenance: The Ford Hill Collection

43 QUEEN ELIZABETH II WITH PRINCE ANDREW AND PRINCE EDWARD, MAY 1964

Signed

Silver gelatin print, printed between 1967 and 1973

15 ¼ x 15 inches

Provenance: The Ford Hill Collection

44 QUEEN ELIZABETH II, OCTOBER 1968
Signed
Silver gelatin print, printed between 1967 and 1973
19 ½ x 15 ½ inches
Provenance: The Ford Hill Collection

CECIL BEATON

45 QUEEN ELIZABETH II, OCTOBER 1968
Signed
C-type print, printed 1972
18 ¾ x 14 ½ inches
Provenance: The Ford Hill Collection

YOUSUF KARSH (1908-2002)

For a biography of Yousuf Karsh, please refer to *The Photographers*, 2010, page 48.

46 QUEEN ELIZABETH II AND PRINCE PHILIP, DUKE OF EDINBURGH, AUGUST 2, 1966
Signed
Silver gelatin print, printed between 1980 and 1985
19 ½ x 15 ½ inches
Provenance: The Ford Hill Collection

47 QUEEN ELIZABETH II, 30 JULY 1951
Signed
Silver gelatin print, printed between 1967 and 1973
19 ½ x 15 ½ inches
Provenance: The Ford Hill Collection

HORST P HORST Horst Paul Albert Bohrmann (1906-1999)

For a biography of Horst P Horst, please refer to *The Photographers 2010*, page 52.

48 LISA WITH TURBAN, PARIS, 1939
Stamped with photographer's blind stamp
Signed and inscribed with title and 'SGP' on reverse
Silver gelatin print, printed later
12 x 9 inches

49 CARMEN FACE MASSAGE, 1949
Stamped with photographer's blind stamp
Signed and inscribed with title and 'SGP' on reverse
Silver gelatin print, printed later
12 x 9 inches

50 WHITE SLEEVE, PARIS, 1936
Stamped with photographer's blind stamp
Signed and inscribed with title on reverse
Silver gelatin print, printed later
22 x 16 ½ inches

GEORGE PLATT LYNES (1907-1955)

George Platt Lynes was an American photographer, whose work remains significant in the history of fashion and portrait photography. He is best known for his celebrity portraits and photographs of the American Ballet Company.

George Platt Lynes was born in East Orange, New Jersey, on 15 April 1907. Having graduated from high school, he was sent to Paris in 1925 by his parents. During this trip he met Gertrude Stein, Glenway Wescott, Monroe Wheeler and other figures who would become significant throughout his career. On his return to America he enrolled at Yale University, but left after one term. He chose instead to set up a bookshop in Englewood, New Jersey; it was at this time that he first became interested in photography, taking photographs of friends to hang in his bookshop. He returned to Paris in 1928, where he stayed for the next three years, in which time he took his earliest celebrity portraits of E M Forster, Tennessee Williams and Jean Cocteau, among others. On his return to America, the art dealer, Julian Levy, gave him his first solo exhibition, held at his gallery in New York. Shortly after, Platt Lynes decided to open his own studio in New York, where many of his fashion and portraiture images were subsequently taken. These photographs were published in several magazines, including *Harper's Bazaar, Town & Country* and *Vogue*.

In 1935, Lincoln Kirstein and George Balanchine asked Platt Lynes to photograph their newly founded American Ballet Company, which he photographed throughout the 1930s and 40s. In 1946 he chose to leave New York for Hollywood, where he was made chief photographer at *Vogue's* California headquarters. As well as his *Vogue* commissions, he photographed notable figures in the film industry during the two years he spent in Hollywood, before returning to New York in 1948. On his return, Platt Lynes did not enjoy the original success he had in the fashion and commercial industry. He turned his attention to more private projects, which he had begun years previously, photographing homoerotic images of male nudes. Man Ray, the surrealist artist he had met in Paris, was a major influence for this project, inspiring his use of theatrical lighting, unconventional angles and poses.

In 1955, Platt Lynes was diagnosed with terminal cancer; he closed his studio in New York and destroyed much of his own archive. Before doing this, however, he privately handed over his photographs of male nudes to Dr Alfred Kinsey, believing them to be his most significant works. This large body of images was rediscovered and published for the first time in 2011.

AM

51 JEAN COCTEAU, 1936
Silver gelatin print, printed circa 1936
9 ½ x 7 ¾ inches

63

HENRI CARTIER-BRESSON (1908-2004)

For a biography of Henri Cartier-Bresson, please refer to *The Photographers 2011*, page 49.

52 PICNIC ON THE BANKS OF THE MARNE, FRANCE, 1938
Signed and stamped with photographer's copyright estate blind stamp
Silver gelatin print, printed later
9 ½ x 14 inches

53 BEHIND THE GARE SAINT-LAZARE, 1932 *(opposite)*
Signed and stamped with photographer's copyright estate blind stamp
Silver gelatin print, printed later
14 x 11 inches

Behind the Gare Saint-Lazare, 1932

Cartier-Bresson published a book in 1952 called *Images à La Sauvette*, which was published in the USA as *The Decisive Moment* – a phrase that has since become intrinsically linked with the photographer and his work. Cartier-Bresson had been an early advocate of the Leica 35mm camera which, at the time, was the most lightweight and therefore portable camera ever made. The great new advantage for a photographer lay in its ease and speed of use, which meant that a significant moment could be captured instantly, with little planning or preparation. Cartier-Bresson pioneered this type of photography, which had obvious application in the developing field of photojournalism. It meant he could respond very quickly to a developing situation, and take pictures that had natural, uncontrived drama.

In the introduction to *The Decisive Moment* he wrote that a photograph should be 'the simultaneous recognition in a fraction of a second of the significance of an event as well as of a precise organization of forms'. However, Cartier-Bresson did not 'point and shoot' to achieve this effect. He often framed a picture in the viewfinder of his Leica, and waited for the perfect event to occur – normally a person passing through the scene. This photograph, *Behind the Gare Saint-Lazare, 1932*, is perhaps the perfect example of this practice, and has subsequently become Cartier-Bresson's most celebrated photograph.

Taken right at the beginning of his career, this photograph is a triumph of technique and new technology. Only with the fast shutter-speed of the Leica could Cartier-Bresson freeze the movement of the man so perfectly, creating the tension between the glassy surface of the water and the splash that will never come.

NORMAN PARKINSON Ronald William Parkinson Smith (1913-1990)

For a biography of Norman Parkinson, please refer to *The Photographers 2010*, page 55.

54 BARBARA MULLEN WEARING JAQUES HEIM,
AT THE RED FORT, DELHI, INDIA, 1956 *(opposite)*
Inscribed 'CV151T-39' by David Searle, Parkinson's assistant and printer on reverse
Silver gelatin print, printed 1956
11 x 11 inches
Client: French *Vogue*
Illustrated: French *Vogue*, 1956, page 102

55 WENDA PARKINSON AND MARLA SCARAFIA
IN MONTE CARLO, 1956
Inscribed 'More Footage'
Inscribed 'p76-25' and 'Wenda+Monte Carlo' on reverse
Silver gelatin print, printed 1956
10 ½ x 15 inches
Client: *Vogue*, 1956

IRVING PENN (1917–2009)

For a biography of Irving Penn, please refer to *The Photographers 2010*, page 56.

Both of these photographs by Irving Penn illustrate his singular ability to produce elegant fashion photographs that are simple, yet also sumptuous and alluring. Penn was the master of studio photography, rarely even deviating from his trademark grey background. Whether in his fashion work, or his significant body of portraiture, Penn's isolation of the subject in this grey expanse meant that there was nothing to distract from the figure in question. Portrait photographers in the years before Penn tended to fill their photographs with sets and props that were intended to reveal something about the sitter. In contrast, most of Penn's pictures have nothing in them except the sitter or model, often in a bare, tatty studio. That they often seem out of place in this odd environment only serves to magnify their personality and presence.

56 FASHION PHOTOGRAPH, (*VOGUE* COVER), NEW YORK, 1951
Signed, inscribed with title, and 'Lisa Fonssagrives-Penn' and stamped with photographer's copyright and edition ink stamps on reverse
Silver gelatin print, printed in 1957 from the colour transparency
7 ½ x 7 ½ inches
From an edition of 6

57 BALENCIAGA, 'LITTLE GREAT' COAT (LISA FONSSAGRIVES-PENN), PARIS, 1950
Signed, inscribed with title, and stamped with photographer's copyright and edition ink stamps on reverse of mount
Selenium toned silver gelatin print, printed in 1985 and mounted on Strathmore paper
14 ½ x 13 inches
From an edition of 16

ROBERT DOISNEAU (1912-1994)

For a biography of Robert Doisneau, please refer to *The Photographers 2010*, page 58

58 LA CONCIERGE AUX
LUNETTES, FRANCE, 1945
Signed
Inscribed with title and dated
on reverse
Silver gelatin print, printed later
12 ½ x 9 ½ inches

SAUL LEITER (born 1923)

Saul Leiter is a self-taught photographer best known for his unique, painterly photographs of the streets of New York City, but he also enjoyed a successful career as a fashion photographer.

Saul Leiter was born in Pittsburgh, Pennsylvania, on 3 December 1923. His father was a well-respected Talmud scholar, and Leiter originally trained to become a Rabbi. When he was 23, however, he left theology school in Cleveland and moved to New York City to become an artist, beginning his career as an abstract painter. In 1946, he met the abstract expressionist Richard Pousette-Dart and the photographer W Eugene Smith, who encouraged him to pursue photography. Inspired by the famous 1947 exhibition of Henri Cartier-Bresson's photographs, held at the Museum of Modern Art, he started to take his own pictures of the streets of New York City, with his 35mm Leica. In 1948, he made his first experiments with colour photography, combining his street photographs with the abstract use of colour from his painting, however he printed very few of these images. As well as his street photography, he also undertook commercial projects, and became a successful fashion photographer, opening his own studio in 1953 on Bleeker Street. That same year, his early photographic work was exhibited in an exhibition organised by Edward Steichen at the Museum of Modern Art. He worked as a fashion photographer for over 20 years, during which time his fashion portraits were published in *Harper's Bazaar, Esquire, Elle* and *Vogue*.

Leiter retained many of his colour photographs, only releasing them in the 1990s. Since this publication the extent of his contribution to colour photography has gained him critical recognition. In 2006 the book, *Early Colour* was published, and two years later the Foundation Henri Cartier-Bresson held Leiter's first solo museum exhibition. His work is included in the permanent collections of the Museum of Modern Art in New York, the Victoria & Albert Museum in London and The Albertina in Vienna.

AM

59 POSTMEN, 1952
Signed on reverse
Digital c-type print, printed later
13 ½ x 9 inches

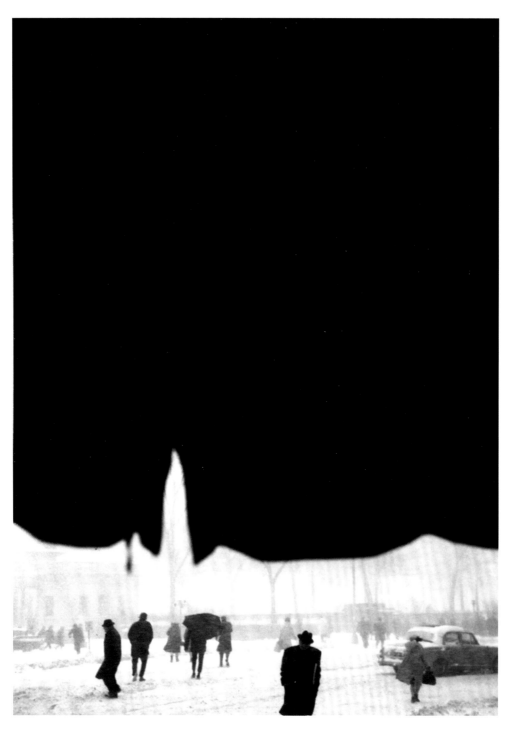

60 CANOPY, 1958
Signed on reverse
Digital c-type print, printed later
13 ½ x 9 inches

61 SNOW, 1960
Signed on reverse
Digital c-type print, printed later
13 ½ x 9 inches

62 HARLEM, 1960
Signed on reverse
Digital c-type print, printed later
13 ½ x 9 inches

MARC RIBOUD (born 1923)

Marc Riboud is one of the most significant contemporary photographers, particularly in the field of documentary photography. His black and white images have been published in *Life*, *National Geographic*, *Paris Match* and *Stern*.

Marc Riboud was born in Lyon, France, on 24 June 1923. He took his first photographs at the age of 14, using his father's Vest Pocket Kodak camera. Active in the French resistance during the Second World War, he then took a degree in engineering at L'École Centrale de Lyon before going on to work in a factory in Villeurbanne. After a week's holiday, which was spent photographing a festival in Lyon, he decided not to return to his job at the factory and focused instead on his photographic work. In 1951 he visited New York for the first time to see the pictures of the American photographers he admired. The following year he moved to Paris, where he met Henri Cartier-Bresson and Robert Capa, who invited him to join Magnum Photos. While living in Paris, he took one of his early iconic photographs of a man posing while painting the Eiffel Tower, which was published in *Life* magazine in 1953.

In 1955 Riboud travelled to India. He spent the following 10 years travelling around Asia, documenting the life and culture of each country he visited including China, Cambodia and Japan. His aim was to capture every aspect of life in these countries; as he believes, 'taking pictures is savouring life intensely, every hundredth of a second.'

The Vietnam War provided him with a new focus and he made three trips to the country, the first in 1968, during which he photographed the effects of the war in both the North and South of the country. He also photographed the reaction to the war in America – his photograph of a young girl confronting police in Washington has become one of the most famous images in the history of photography. In 1976 he became president of Magnum Photos, a position he held for three years before leaving the organisation and continuing his travels in Europe.

Riboud has also made numerous portraits of significant figures in both the political and artistic fields, most recently documenting the election of Barack Obama in America. His photographs are held in the permanent collections of the Museum of Modern Art in New York, and the Victoria and Albert Museum in London.

AM

63 CONFRONTATION BETWEEN A FLOWER AND THE BAYONETS OF SOLDIERS GUARDING THE PENTAGON DURING THE MARCH FOR PEACE IN VIETNAM, WASHINGTON DC, 1967
Signed
Stamped with photographer's address ink stamp on reverse
Silver gelatin print, printed later
9 ½ x 14 ¼ inches

64 EIFFEL TOWER,
PARIS, 1953
Signed and dated
Stamped with photographer's
address ink stamp on reverse
Silver gelatin print, printed later
14 ¼ x 9 ½ inches

HERMAN LEONARD (1923-2010)

Herman Leonard was an American photographer whose smoky, atmospheric images of New York's jazz scene in the 1950s helped to record and define a remarkable period in popular music.

Herman Leonard was born in Allentown, Pennsylvania, on 6 March 1923 to Joseph Leonard and Rose Morrison, both immigrants from Romania. An early fascination with photography led him to study the subject at Ohio University, and he received his Bachelor of Fine Arts degree in 1947. After graduating, Leonard became an apprentice for the renowned portrait photographer, Yousuf Karsh, whose finely-honed studio technique had a lasting influence on him. Karsh encouraged Leonard to pursue a career as a photographer, and with his blessing he moved to New York in 1948 to open his own photography studio.

Once in New York, Leonard was able to enjoy another passion – jazz. During the day he would work as a freelance photographer at his Greenwich Village studio, and at night he would frequent the key jazz clubs of the day, namely The Royal Roost, Birdland and Bop City. Leonard developed relationships with the managers of the clubs, arranging free entry in return for taking photographs that the club could use in their publicity. Leonard's timing couldn't have been better, as New York had become the centre of the jazz world during the late 1940s, drawing great stars such as Dizzy Gillespie, Charlie Parker, Thelonius Monk and others to perform there. Leonard became a regular face at the clubs with his Speed Graphic camera, and the photographs that he took – black and white, smoky, moodily lit and candid – became key images of this remarkable period in the history of jazz. He also became life-long friends with many of the musicians, including Tony Bennett and Quincy Jones.

Leonard left New York in the late 1950s, pursuing the jazz scene to Paris where he lived until 1980. A brief period living in Ibiza preceded a move to New Orleans in 1992. During this time Leonard continued to photograph jazz musicians, but also branched out into fashion, travel and other types of commercial photography.

In the mid 1980s Leonard began to promote his unique archive of jazz images, staging exhibitions around the world and publishing books such as *The Eye of Jazz* in 1985 and *Jazz Memories* in 1995. In 2005 Hurricane Katrina destroyed most of Leonard's home and studio, including more than 8000 prints. His negatives, which were stored in a vault, remained unscathed. A Grammy Foundation Grant in 2008 enabled him to organise and digitise this archive, which is now fully catalogued for posterity. Leonard continued to be actively involved with music photography, and was the official photographer of the Montreal Jazz Festival in 2009.

Herman Leonard died in Los Angeles on 14 August 2010 from a short illness. He was married three times, and is survived by his four children and six grandchildren. GHP

65 'PREZ' LESTER YOUNG, NYC, 1948
Signed, inscribed with title, dated and numbered 36/50
Signed, inscribed with title, photographer's copyright details, and 'LSY3',
dated and numbered 36/50 on reverse
Silver gelatin print, printed later
14 ½ x 13 ½ inches
From an edition of 50

66 MILES DAVIES, NYC, 1949
Signed, inscribed with title, dated and numbered 1/50
Signed, inscribed with title and photographer's copyright details,
dated and numbered on reverse
Silver gelatin print, printed later
16 ½ x 14 ¾ inches
From an edition of 50

67 MILES DAVIES, NYC, 1953
Signed, inscribed with title, dated and numbered 1/50
Signed, inscribed with title and photographer's copyright details, dated and
numbered on reverse
Silver gelatin print, printed later
13 ½ x 18 inches
From an edition of 50

68 DUKE ELLINGTON,
PARIS, 1958
Signed, inscribed with title, dated
and numbered 35/50
Signed, inscribed with title, dated
and numbered 35/50 on reverse
Silver gelatin print, printed later
17 ¾ x 14 ½ inches
From an edition of 50

DENNIS STOCK (1928-2010)

Dennis Stock, an American documentary photographer best known for his glamorous photographs of American icons of the 1950s to 1970s, enjoyed a long and diverse career as a member of Magnum Photos. His pictures have been published in such magazines as *Life*, *Stern* and *Paris Match*.

Dennis Stock was born in New York on 24 July 1928, to a Swiss father and a British mother. Leaving home at the age of 16 to join the US Navy, Stock gave up his military career in 1947 and took up an apprenticeship under Gjon Mili, a photographer at *Life*. He achieved early success in his career winning the *Life* magazine Young Photographers award in 1951 and becoming a full member of Magnum in 1954. A year later he went on to produce arguably the most famous work of his career when he took a series of photographs of the young Hollywood icon, James Dean walking through a rain-drenched Times Square.

Stock is also well known for the series of photographs he took of jazz musicians from 1957 until 1961, including important figures such as Louis Armstrong and Sidney Bechet. In 1968 Stock took a brief interlude from working with Magnum to start his own company, Visual Objectives Inc, which produced several documentaries. A year later, however, Stock returned to Magnum as President of the new Media and Film Department.

The 1970s and 1980s saw a change of direction in Stock's career. Moving to Provence in France, Stock set about photographing the landscape and nature around his new home. He died in Sarasota, Florida, on 11 January 2010.

AM

69 AUDREY HEPBURN, DURING THE FILMING OF *SABRINA*, 1954
Signed on reverse
Silver gelatin print, printed later
18 ½ x 12 ¼ inches

70 JAMES DEAN, TIMES
SQUARE, NEW YORK, 1955
Signed on reverse
Silver gelatin print, printed later
12 ¾ x 9 inches

ROGER MAYNE (born 1929)

For a biography of Roger Mayne, please refer to *The Photographers 2010*, page 82.

71 CHILDREN IN BOMBED BUILDING, BERMONDSEY, 1954
Signed and dated '54 and '*'08'
Inscribed 'CU2' on reverse
Silver gelatin print, printed 2008
14 ½ x 9 ½ inches

72 FOOTBALLER REACHING, BRINDLEY ROAD, 1957
Signed and dated '57 and '*'02'
Signed, inscribed with title and dated on reverse
Silver gelatin print, printed 2002
13 ½ x 10 ¼ inches

73 GROUP IN THE ROAD, ST STEPHENS GARDENS, LONDON W2, 1957

Signed and dated '57 and '*'91'

Signed, inscribed with title and dated on reverse

Silver gelatin print, printed 1991

12 ¾ x 17 inches

ALBERT WATSON (born 1942)

Albert Watson is one of the most successful contemporary fashion and commercial photographers. His extensive archive of fashion and celebrity portraits has been published in magazines such as *GQ, Vogue, Harper's Bazaar* and *Rolling Stone.*

Albert Watson was born in Edinburgh, Scotland. He studied graphic design at the Duncan of Jordanstone College of Art and Design in Dundee, before moving to London, where he received a degree from the Royal College of Art, specialising in film and television. In 1970, he moved to America with his wife, Elizabeth, and took up photography as a hobby. Later that year, he was given his first test session by Max Factor, who subsequently used two of his prints. In 1976 he was commissioned for his first *Vogue* cover. Since then he has photographed more than 250 covers for the magazine all over the world, as well as making numerous advertising campaigns, film and television work. Many of his portraits have become iconic images of the public figures they depict, from rappers and models to members of the British Royal Family. Throughout his career in the fashion and commercial industry, he has also worked on a portfolio of his personal work. These projects document his travels in Morocco, Las Vegas and Scotland and have been published in several books.

In 2010 Watson was awarded the Centenary Medal by the Royal Photographic Society and his work now forms part of the permanent collections at The National Portrait Gallery, London, and The Metropolitan Museum, New York.

AM

74 CHRISTY TURLINGTON, NEW YORK, 1990
Signed and inscribed with title on reverse
Silver gelatin print, printed later
14 x 10 ¾ inches

75 MONKEY WITH GUN, NEW YORK, 1992

Signed and inscribed with title on reverse

Silver gelatin print, printed later

20 x 24 inches

76 MIKE TYSON, NEW YORK, 1986 (*opposite*)

Signed and inscribed with title on reverse

Silver gelatin print, printed later

12 ¾ x 10 ½ inches

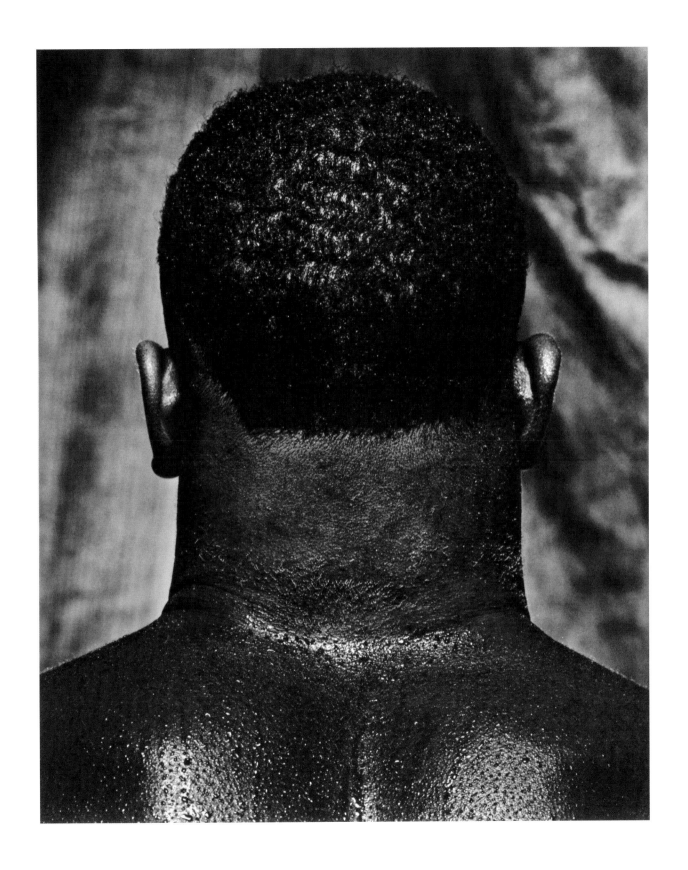

77 MICK JAGGER, 1992
Signed and inscribed
with title on reverse
Silver gelatin print,
printed later
12 ¾ x 10 ¼ inches

78 ALFRED HITCHCOCK,
LOS ANGELES, 1973
Signed and inscribed with title
on reverse
Silver gelatin print, printed later
14 x 11 inches

SARAH QUILL Sarah Penelope Quill (born 1946)

For a biography of Sarah Quill, please refer to *The Photographers 2011*, page 114.

79 PROCURATIE VECCHIE WITH BANNERS, VENICE, 1993

Signed, inscribed with title and numbered

Inscribed with printing date on reverse of mount

Digital c-type print, mounted on board, printed 2012

14 x 20 inches

From an edition of 25

80 INTERIOR, CA' D'ORO, VENICE, 2004 *(opposite)*

Signed, inscribed with title and numbered

Inscribed with printing date on reverse of mount

Digital fibre print, mounted on board, printed 2012

20 x 15 inches

From an edition of 25

81 RIO DELLA GIUDECCA, BURANO, 2010 (*inverted image*)

Signed, inscribed with title and numbered

Inscribed with printing date on reverse of mount

Digital c-type print, mounted on board, printed 2012

15 x 20 inches

From an edition of 25

82 FRATELLI IN PIAZZA GALUPPI, BURANO, 2010

Signed, inscribed with title and numbered

Digital fibre print, mounted on board, printed 2012

14 ½ x 20 inches

From an edition of 25

SEBASTIAO SALGADO (born 1944)

For a biography of Sebastião Salgado, please refer to *The Photographers 2011*, page 108.

83 REFUGEES AT THE KOREM CAMP, ETHIOPIA, 1984
Stamped with photographer's copyright blind stamp
Signed on reverse
Silver gelatin print, printed later
Printed on 20 x 24 inch paper

84 SAND DUNE, NAMIBIA, 2005
Signed and inscribed with title on reverse
Silver gelatin print, printed later
Printed on 24 x 35 inch paper

85 PENGUINS, ANTARCTICA, 2005
Signed and inscribed with title on reverse
Silver gelatin print, printed later
Printed on 24 x 35 inch paper

86 ALTO XINGO INDIANS, AMAZONAS, BRAZIL, 2005
Signed and inscribed with title on reverse
Silver gelatin print, printed later
Printed on 24 x 35 inch paper

STEVE MCCURRY (born 1950)

For a biography of Steve McCurry, please refer to *The Photographers 2011*, page 106.

87 CAMELS IN DUST STORM, INDIA, 2010
Signed, affixed with photographer's edition label and numbered on reverse
Digital c-type print, printed 2012
Printed on 20 x 24 inch paper
From an edition of 75

88 ROAD TO JALALABAD, AFGHANISTAN, 1992
Signed, affixed with photographer's edition label and numbered on reverse
Digital c-type print, printed 2012
Printed on 20 x 24 inch paper
From an edition of 30

89 THE BLUE CITY, INDIA, 2010

Signed, affixed with photographer's edition label and numbered on reverse

Digital c-type print, printed 2012

Printed on 20 x 24 inch paper

From an edition of 75

90 MARKET VENDORS ON DAL LAKE, KASHMIR, 1999
Signed, affixed with photographer's edition label and numbered on reverse
Digital c-type print, printed 2012
Printed on 20 x 24 inch paper
From an edition of 30

OLAF OTTO BECKER (born 1952)

Olaf Otto Becker follows in the tradition of Herbert Ponting and William Bradford, early photographers who travelled to the polar regions to photograph these dramatic and unexplored landscapes. Like his predecessors, Becker aims to find a balance between both the artistic and the scientific in his photography.

Olaf Otto Becker was born in Lübeck, Germany, in 1959. In 1981 he went to study Communication Design in Augsburg, Germany. It was at this point that his interest in photography grew. He was also a keen amateur painter.

The first images Becker took were of the landscape around his home in Germany, before travelling further abroad to develop his photography. In particular, he visited Iceland and Greenland as he was drawn by the quality of light. There Becker aimed to find landscapes that had little human interference: 'I was interested in a wild, unspoiled landscape. I was interested in a place where the landscape developed on its own'. He travelled overland and by boat to photograph the glaciers and icebergs on the islands on his large-format (8x10 inch) camera.

He has most recently completed *Under the Nordic Light*, in which he photographed Iceland from 1999-2011. In this project Becker's main objective was to photograph changes in the landscape as it is impacted by both man and global warming. His work has won him several awards, including the Deutscher Fotobuchpreis in 2007.

Becker has had the results of his travels published in several books, and his work has been exhibited in numerous galleries and museums in New York, Amsterdam, Los Angeles, Munich and Seoul.

AM

91 INLAND ICE 5, 07/2007
Affixed with photographer's signature label on reverse
Archival pigment print, printed 2012
18 ¾ x 23 ½ inches

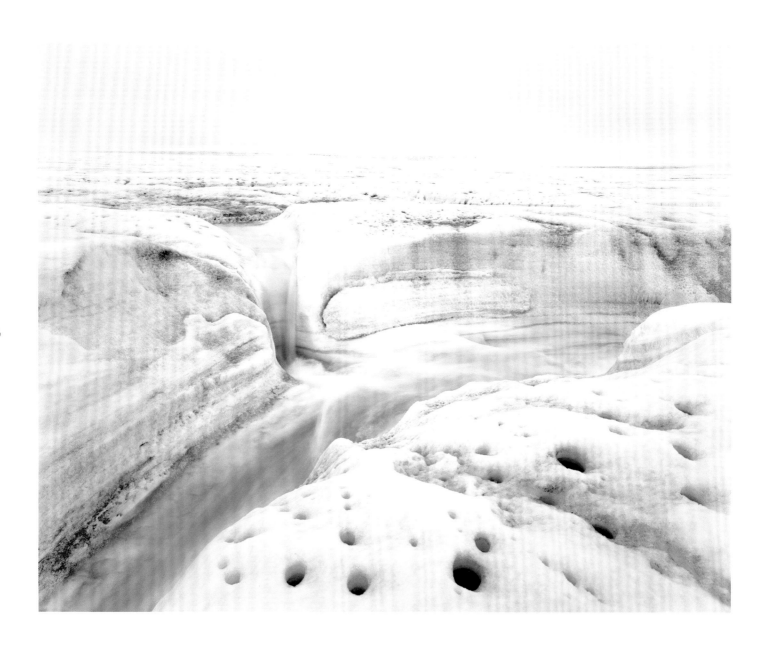

92 ABOVE ZERO, RIVER 2, 07, 2008, POSITION 1
Affixed with photographer's signature label on reverse
Archival pigment print, printed 2012
18 ¾ x 23 ½ inches

93 ABOVE ZERO, RIVER 1, 07, 2007, POSITION 13
Affixed with photographer's signature label on reverse
Archival pigment print, printed 2012
18 ¾ x 23 ½ inches

ABELARDO MORELL (born 1948)

Abelardo Morell is one of the most respected Amercian photographers in the field of contemporary photography, known for his innovative working methods that often include the use of a Camera Obscura.

Abelardo Morell was born in Havana, Cuba, on 17 September 1948. When he was 14 years old he fled with his family to America, where they settled in New York. He graduated in 1977 with a BA in Fine Art from Bowdoin College, Maine, and went on to gain an MA in Fine Art from Yale University School of Art in 1981.

His earliest photographs were taken in his darkened living room, in 1991. Using a Camera Obscura technique, Morell produced black and white images of interiors that reflect a view of their outdoor surroundings. Allowing a small ray of light to shine into the unlit room from outside, he then captures the reflection on his large-format camera, often exposing the film for up to eight hours. He is drawn to this traditional technique of photography as he enjoys 'seeing the weird and yet natural marriage of the inside and outside'. From the interior spaces of his own home, he went on to create many more of these Camera Obscura images in rooms all over the world. In 1995 the first collection of these pictures was published in a book, *A Camera in a Room*. Other early works focus on household objects that he examines in extreme close-up, showing the viewer a familiar object at an unusual angle. While his style has remained unchanged, in his various projects he has photographed books, maps, people and works of art.

Morell's recent images evolve from his early subject matter, which he now photographs in colour. Last year he received the Infinity Award from the International Center of Photography in New York. He is also a professor of art at the Massachusetts College of Art in Boston.

Morell's work has been exhibited in some of the most renowned galleries and museums in the world, including the Victoria & Albert museum, London, the Whitney Museum of American Art and the Metropolitan Museum of Art, New York.

AM

The Camera Obscura

The Camera Obscura, literally meaning 'dark chamber,' has a long history and is considered an ancestor of the camera. In its simplest form the Camera Obscura is just a sealed box with a single small hole, through which a beam of light shines, reflecting an upside-down image on the opposite side – this is exactly the technique used by Abelardo Morell, except that he uses a room, not a box.

The Camera Obscura process was first described as early as the 4th Century BC by Aristotle in Ancient Greece, but came to prominence during the Renaissance when artists commonly used it as a tool in their drawing and painting work to trace the outline of a figure or landscape. By the 18th Century, the Camera Obscura had proved so useful that a portable device was invented, in order for it to be used by artists whilst travelling. It consisted of a small, wooden box, constructed following the designs of Robert Boyle and Robert Hooke, which contained a lens and a mirror to right the upside-down image.

In the 19th Century the Camera Obscura system led to the invention of modern photography. Henry Fox Talbot, an English pioneer of the medium, created light sensitive paper to record an image passed through a lens, while simultaneously Louis-Jacques-Mandé Dagguere and Joseph Nicéphore Niépce, in France, invented a similar photographic technique. Both of the systems were founded on the principle of the Camera Obscura.

94 CAMERA OBSCURA: IMAGE OF THE COLISEUM INSIDE ROOM NO 20 AT THE HOTEL GLADITORI, 2007
Signed, dated, inscribed with title and numbered on reverse
Archival pigment print, mounted on aluminium, printed 2010
30 x 24 inches
From an edition of 10

95 CAMERA OBSCURA: VIEW OF LANDSCAPE OUTSIDE FLORENCE
IN ROOM WITH BOOKS, 2010

Signed, dated, inscribed with title and numbered on reverse

Archival pigment print, mounted on aluminium, printed 2010

24 x 30 inches

From an edition of 10

96 CAMERA OBSCURA: GARDEN WITH OLIVE TREE INSIDE ROOM
WITH PLANTS, ITALY, 2009
Signed, dated, inscribed with title and numbered on reverse
Archival pigment print, mounted on aluminium, printed 2010
24 x 30 inches
From an edition of 10

97 CAMERA OBSCURA: VIEW OF THE LANDSCAPE OUTSIDE FLORENCE
LOOKING EAST TOWARD WHERE GALILEO LIVED, ITALY, 2009
Signed, dated, inscribed with title and numbered on reverse
Archival pigment print, mounted on aluminium, printed 2010
30 x 24 inches
From an edition of 10

JULIA FULLERTON-BATTEN (born 1970)

Julia Fullerton-Batten is a British contemporary photographer, known for her elaborate projects that reference her own upbringing and life-experience.

Julia Fullerton-Batten was born in Bremen, Germany, to an English father and German mother. The second of four siblings, she lived in Germany and America before moving to England when her parents divorced. As a teenager Fullerton-Batten experimented with her father's SLR camera, and was enthused by photography enough to study the subject at the Royal Berkshire College of Art and Design.

After graduating, Fullerton-Batten spent five years as a photographer's assistant in London, before being taken on in her own right by a German photographic agent.

While developing an enviable portfolio of commissions, Fullerton-Batten has also pursued a number of elaborate personal projects that have been exhibited in museums and galleries worldwide. Drawing on her own memories her pictures are often concerned with female adolescence, and the awkwardness and isolation associated with school, relationships and the passage into adulthood. Large in both scale and concept, and often unsettling, Fullerton-Batten's projects such as 'Teenage Stories' (2005), 'School Play' (2007), 'In Between' (2008-2009), 'Awkward' (2011) and 'Mothers & Daughters' (2012), feature elaborately staged set-pieces imbued with tension and a hint of mystery. Her most recent project, 'Unadorned' (2012) addresses the issue of beauty and pride in overweight people, featuring a series of nudes that recreate the palette and composition of Old Master Paintings.

Julia Fullerton-Batten lives and works in London.

GHP

98 HALLWAY, 2008
Signed, and numbered
on reverse
Digital c-type print
31 x 25 inches
from an edition of 15
54 x 40 inches
from an edition of 7

LOTTIE DAVIES (born 1971)

Lottie Davies is a British contemporary photographer, who is known for her elaborately constructed, thought-provoking, large-scale photographic projects.

Lottie Davies was born in Guildford, Surrey. When she was 14 years old, her father purchased a darkroom kit for her brother, which Davies began to experiment with as well. Although she chose to study philosophy at St Andrews University, she continued to practise with photography and was frequently asked to take the theatre stills and publicity photographs for productions staged at the university theatre. In 1995 she moved to London, having decided to pursue a career in photography and for the next five years she worked as a an assistant at hire studios and for individual photographers.

In 2000 Davies started her own independent photographic work in earnest. Her earliest projects include, *Lights in the Trees*, *Myths* and *Unseen World*, all of which were inspired by a range of stories, personal histories and memories. Her experience with theatre and stage management has been a major influence in her art, which is always meticulously planned and researched – indeed she often uses actors in photographs to embody the characters she wishes to portray.

She is currently preparing her latest project, *Love Stories* – a series of large-scale images recounting the story of how couples first met. Davies has exhibited her work in America, Italy and France and continues to shoot commercial projects including food and travel photography. Her work is regularly published in magazines, newspapers and catalogues and used in advertisements.

AM

99 EX CAELO LUX:
TWENTY-ONE
CHINESE LANTERNS
Signed, inscribed with title
and numbered
Digital c-type print
20 x 24 inches –
from an edition of 20
30 x 40 inches –
from an edition of 6

100 EX CAELO LUX: SEVENTY-ONE CANDLES IN JAM JARS

Signed, inscribed with title and numbered

Digital c-type print

20 x 24 inches – from an edition of 20

30 x 40 inches – from an edition of 6

MATTHEW PILLSBURY (born 1973)

Matthew Pillsbury is a leading contemporary photographer, who is well known for his depictions of New York life.

Matthew Pillsbury was born in Neuilly, France, on 25 November 1973 to American parents, who had moved to France in the 1960s. Pillsbury was educated in France, before moving to America in 1991, where he graduated from Yale University School of Art with a BA in Fine Art in 1995. It was at Yale, studying under Lois Conner, that he first became interested in photography as an art form. His career began when *The New York Times* commissioned him to make a series of photographs of New York museums after closing time. In 2005 he began his next project, *Screen Lives,* which would preoccupy him for several years. Inspired by his interest in how technology influences our lives, Pillsbury set about photographing friends and family using computers and watching television in their apartments. The latter was a novel activity for him, as his parents had not allowed him to watch it as a child.

Pillsbury uses a large format 8x10 inch camera to produce the black and white photographs, which he exposes for up to two hours – giving the picture a ghostly appearance. This technique is similar to that of Abelardo Morell, a photographer and fellow Yale alumni, who has been a key influence on him throughout his career.

In his most recent project, *City Stages,* he focuses his lens on events at iconic locations around New York City, such as jazz performances at The Lincoln Centre, and a Chinese New Year parade through Chinatown. The project received critical acclaim, and several prints from the series were printed in *New York Magazine* in 2011 for a feature called *Reasons to Love New York 2011*. His photographs are included in the permanent collections of over 20 museums and galleries including The Museum of Modern Art and The Whitney Museum of American Art, New York, as well as both The Louvre, Paris and Tate Modern, London. AM

101 SITTING ON THE HIGH LINE, THURSDAY, 10 NOVEMBER 2011
Signed, inscribed with title , dated and numbered 1/10
Archival pigment print, printed 2011
on 30 x 40 inch paper
From an edition of 10

102 VICTORIAN GARDEN, NEW YORK, 2012
Signed, inscribed with title , dated and numbered 1/10
Archival pigment print, printed 2012
on 30 x 40 inch paper
From an edition of 10